Heat Changes Things

by Michael Medearis

Contents

Harcourt

Orlando   Boston   Dallas   Chicago   San Diego

www.harcourtschool.com

It's a hot day.
I want a cold drink.
So, I put ice in my drink.
Then,

I set my cold drink
in the sun while I go
inside for a snack.

A cheese sandwich looks good. So, I put cheese on the bread. Then,

4

Mom turns on the heat.
The heat melts the cheese.

The heat changes
the bread, too.

I think some popcorn
will taste good, too.
So, I put the popcorn
in the popper. Then,

the heat helps
the popcorn pop.

Heat helped me fix lunch. I am glad heat changes things!

Oops! Heat has melted my ice.

Glossary

heat

melt

Index